The look again... and again, and again, and again book.

Sails

Crab claws

Banana split

Parrot's beak

Text and graphics by Beau Gardner

Lothrop, Lee & Shepard Books, New York

Printed in the United States of America.
First Edition
1 2 3 4 5 6 7 8 9 10

Library of Congress Cataloging in Publication Data
Gardner, Beau.
The look again—and again and again and again book.

Summary: By turning the book four different ways,
the reader may view the graphics of familiar objects and
gain a different perception each time.
1. Visual perception—Juvenile literature.
2. Picture perception—Juvenile literature.
[1. Visual perception. 2. Toy and movable books]
I. Title.
BF241.G27   1984   153.7   84-748
ISBN 0-688-03805-0
ISBN 0-688-03806-9 (lib. bdg.)

Other books illustrated by Beau Gardner:
The turn about, think about, look about book
The Upside Down Riddle Book, compiled by Louis Phillips

Introduction

This is a book that invites you to enjoy it in more ways than one. As the title implies, if you look at one image, then turn the book on its side and look again, you will see a different image. Each picture can be looked at four different ways. Or, use your imagination to give each picture your own title.

Beau Gardner

BDY

Hot dogs on a grill

Truck carrying rubber rafts

Stop

Invitation to shake hands

Peas in a pod

Hippo's smile

Giraffe passing by a window

Finger holding fish hook

Flower vase

Antique car horn

Key hole

Inside the letter "C"

Pipe bowl

Woody Woodpecker laughing

A hungry baby bird

Bear's claw

Falling Christmas tree

Running out of a cave

Running into a cave

Jumping into a hole

Number four

Sun and pyramid

Owl winking

Ball falling off table

Curtain

Stairs

Fence

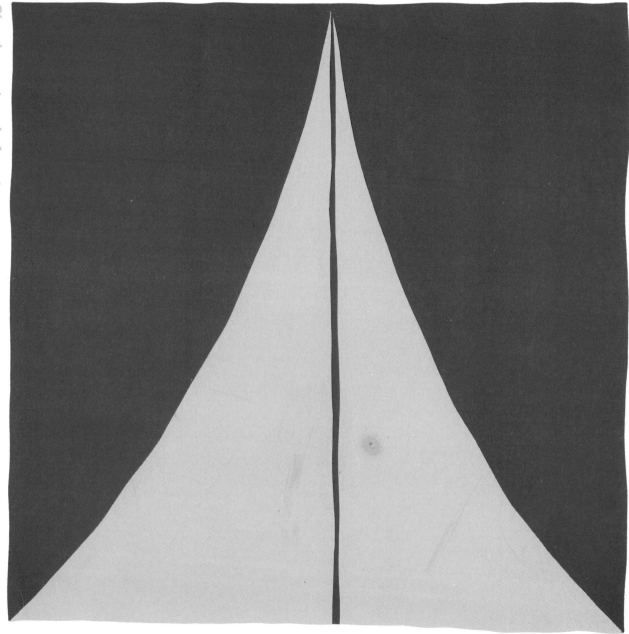

Slurping a strand of pasta

Mountain meets the lake

Tent

Two pointed hats

Ice-cream cones

Two straws

Yellow brick road

Elephant's trunk

Close-up view of all-day sucker